Artificial Intelligence and Ethics

Navigating the Future of Technology

by Rakesh Chittineni

ISBN:

9798333005953

First Edition

Introduction

The Rise of Artificial Intelligence

Brief History and Rapid Development of AI Technology

Artificial Intelligence (AI) has transitioned from a speculative concept in science fiction to a transformative force shaping various aspects of modern life. The journey of AI began in the mid-20th century with the pioneering work of computer scientists like Alan Turing, who proposed the idea of machines simulating human intelligence. The term "Artificial Intelligence" was officially coined in 1956 during the Dartmouth Conference, which is considered the birthplace of AI as an academic discipline.

The early years of AI were marked by optimism and significant breakthroughs, such as the development of early neural networks and symbolic AI. However, the field faced several setbacks during the "AI winters" of the 1970s and 1980s, periods characterized by reduced funding and interest due to the slow progress and unmet expectations.

The resurgence of AI began in the late 1990s and early 2000s, driven by advancements in computing power, the availability of large datasets, and improvements in machine learning algorithms. Notable milestones include IBM's Deep Blue defeating world chess champion Garry Kasparov in 1997 and the advent of Google's search engine, which utilized early AI techniques for web indexing and ranking.

The past decade has witnessed an exponential growth in AI capabilities, largely fueled by deep learning—a subset of machine learning that leverages multi-layered neural networks to analyze vast amounts of data. This era has given rise to AI systems capable of surpassing human performance in tasks such as image recognition, natural language processing, and complex strategy games, exemplified by DeepMind's AlphaGo defeating a world champion Go player in 2016.

Examples of AI in Everyday Life

AI has seamlessly integrated into our daily lives, often in ways that we may not even realize. Here are some prominent examples:

1. **Virtual Assistants**: AI-powered virtual assistants like Apple's Siri, Amazon's Alexa, and Google Assistant have become ubiquitous, helping users with tasks ranging from setting reminders to controlling smart home devices.
2. **Recommendation Systems**: Streaming services like Netflix and Spotify use AI algorithms to analyze user preferences and suggest movies, TV shows, and music, enhancing the user experience through personalized recommendations.
3. **Autonomous Vehicles**: Self-driving cars, developed by companies like Tesla and Waymo, leverage AI to navigate roads, interpret traffic signals, and avoid obstacles, promising to revolutionize transportation by improving safety and efficiency.

4. **Healthcare**: AI is transforming healthcare by assisting in diagnostic imaging, predicting patient outcomes, and personalizing treatment plans. For example, AI algorithms can analyze medical images to detect diseases like cancer with high accuracy.
5. **Finance**: In the financial sector, AI-driven systems are used for fraud detection, algorithmic trading, and personalized banking services, enhancing both security and customer satisfaction.
6. **Customer Service**: AI chatbots and virtual agents handle customer inquiries, provide support, and resolve issues in real-time, improving efficiency and reducing wait times for customers.

The Importance of Ethical Considerations

Why Ethics Matter in the Development and Deployment of AI

As AI continues to permeate various aspects of society, the importance of ethical considerations cannot be overstated. The development and deployment of AI systems come with significant responsibilities, as these technologies have the potential to impact billions of lives. Ethical AI is not merely about adhering to regulations but ensuring that AI technologies are developed and used in ways that are fair, transparent, and beneficial to all.

Overview of Key Ethical Concerns Related to AI

1. **Bias and Fairness**: AI systems learn from data, and if that data reflects existing biases, the AI can perpetuate and even amplify those biases. This can lead to unfair treatment of individuals or groups, particularly in sensitive areas such as hiring, law enforcement, and lending.
2. **Privacy and Surveillance**: AI technologies often rely on large amounts of personal data. Ensuring that this data is collected, stored, and used responsibly is crucial to protect individuals' privacy. There is also a fine line between beneficial surveillance (e.g., for security purposes) and intrusive monitoring that infringes on civil liberties.
3. **Accountability and Transparency**: AI decision-making processes can be opaque, making it difficult to understand how and why certain decisions are made. This "black box" nature of AI necessitates mechanisms for accountability and transparency to ensure that AI systems can be scrutinized and held responsible for their actions.
4. **Autonomy and Control**: As AI systems become more autonomous, questions arise about the extent of control humans should retain over these systems. Ensuring that humans remain in the loop and can override AI decisions when necessary is essential to maintain safety and ethical standards.
5. **Impact on Employment**: The automation potential of AI poses significant challenges to the workforce, with many jobs at risk of being displaced. Addressing these challenges through policies that support retraining and transition for affected workers is crucial for societal stability.
6. **Security and Safety**: AI systems can be vulnerable to attacks and manipulations, posing risks to safety and security. Ensuring robust security measures and developing AI systems that can withstand adversarial attacks is vital.

In summary, the rise of artificial intelligence brings unprecedented opportunities but also profound ethical challenges. Navigating these challenges requires a collective effort from technologists, policymakers, ethicists, and society at large to ensure that AI serves as a force for good. This book aims to explore these ethical considerations in depth, providing insights and recommendations for fostering responsible AI development and deployment.

Chapter 1: Understanding Artificial Intelligence

What is AI?

Definition and Different Types of AI

Artificial Intelligence (AI) refers to the simulation of human intelligence in machines that are programmed to think, learn, and adapt like humans. These machines can perform tasks that typically require human intelligence, such as visual perception, speech recognition, decision-making, and language translation.

AI can be categorized into two main types: Narrow AI and General AI.

1) **Narrow AI**:
   a) Also known as Weak AI, Narrow AI is designed to perform a specific task or a narrow set of tasks. These systems are highly specialized and operate under predefined parameters. Examples include virtual assistants like Siri and Alexa, recommendation algorithms used by Netflix and Amazon, and image recognition systems.
   b) Narrow AI is prevalent today and has achieved significant success in various applications, but it lacks generalization beyond its specific domain.
2) **General AI**:
   a) Also known as Strong AI or Artificial General Intelligence (AGI), General AI refers to systems with the ability to understand, learn, and apply knowledge across a wide range of tasks at a level comparable to human intelligence. AGI would possess the capability to perform any intellectual task that a human can do.
   b) General AI remains theoretical at this stage, with researchers striving to overcome numerous scientific and technical challenges to achieve it.

Key Components of AI

1) **Machine Learning**:
   a) Machine Learning (ML) is a subset of AI that focuses on developing algorithms that enable computers to learn from and make decisions based on data. Unlike traditional programming, where explicit instructions are given, ML algorithms identify patterns in data and improve their performance over time.
   b) There are three main types of machine learning: supervised learning, unsupervised learning, and reinforcement learning.
      i) **Supervised Learning**: Algorithms are trained on labeled data, meaning that each training example is paired with an output label. The model learns to predict the output from the input data.
      ii) **Unsupervised Learning**: Algorithms are used on data without labeled responses, identifying hidden patterns or intrinsic structures in the data.
      iii) **Reinforcement Learning**: Algorithms learn to make decisions by taking actions in an environment to maximize some notion of cumulative reward.

2) **Neural Networks**:
   a) Neural networks are a series of algorithms that attempt to recognize underlying relationships in a set of data through a process that mimics the way the human brain operates. They consist of layers of interconnected nodes, or neurons, where each connection represents a synapse.
   b) Neural networks are the foundation of deep learning and are particularly effective for tasks such as image and speech recognition.
3) **Deep Learning**:
   a) Deep Learning is a subset of machine learning that uses neural networks with many layers (hence "deep") to model complex patterns in large datasets. It has revolutionized fields such as computer vision, natural language processing, and speech recognition.
   b) Deep learning models, such as convolutional neural networks (CNNs) and recurrent neural networks (RNNs), have achieved state-of-the-art performance in various tasks by automatically extracting hierarchical features from raw data.

Applications of AI

Current Uses in Various Sectors

1. **Healthcare**:
   a. **Diagnostics**: AI algorithms analyze medical images, such as X-rays, MRIs, and CT scans, to detect diseases like cancer with high accuracy. For example, Google's DeepMind has developed AI models that can diagnose eye diseases from retinal scans.
   b. **Personalized Medicine**: AI helps in tailoring treatment plans based on individual patient data, including genetic information, lifestyle, and medical history. This approach enhances the effectiveness of treatments and reduces adverse effects.
   c. **Predictive Analytics**: AI models predict patient outcomes and disease progression, aiding in early intervention and preventive care.
2. **Finance**:
   a. **Fraud Detection**: AI systems analyze transaction patterns to detect fraudulent activities in real-time, safeguarding financial institutions and customers.
   b. **Algorithmic Trading**: AI algorithms analyze market data and execute trades at high speeds and frequencies, optimizing investment strategies and maximizing returns.
   c. **Customer Service**: AI-powered chatbots and virtual assistants provide instant support to customers, answering queries and resolving issues efficiently.
3. **Education**:
   a. **Personalized Learning**: AI systems adapt educational content to individual student needs, providing customized learning experiences and improving outcomes.
   b. **Automated Grading**: AI tools assist educators by automatically grading assignments and exams, saving time and ensuring consistency.

     c. **Student Support**: AI chatbots offer 24/7 assistance to students, answering questions about course content, administrative procedures, and more.
4. **Entertainment**:
     a. **Content Recommendations**: AI algorithms analyze user preferences and behaviors to recommend movies, TV shows, music, and other content, enhancing user engagement on platforms like Netflix and Spotify.
     b. **Content Creation**: AI tools assist in creating content, such as generating music, writing articles, and designing graphics, pushing the boundaries of creativity.

Potential Future Applications and Innovations

1. **Smart Cities**:
     a. AI can optimize urban planning, traffic management, and energy consumption in smart cities. Intelligent transportation systems can reduce congestion, while AI-powered utilities can enhance energy efficiency and sustainability.
2. **Agriculture**:
     a. AI-driven precision farming techniques can improve crop yields, optimize resource usage, and reduce environmental impact. AI can monitor soil health, predict weather patterns, and automate tasks like planting and harvesting.
3. **Customer Experience**:
     a. AI will continue to revolutionize customer service by providing more sophisticated virtual assistants capable of understanding and responding to complex queries. AI-driven sentiment analysis can enhance customer satisfaction by tailoring interactions based on emotional context.
4. **Advanced Robotics**:
     a. Future AI advancements will lead to more capable and autonomous robots that can perform complex tasks in diverse environments, from manufacturing and logistics to healthcare and household chores.
5. **Environmental Protection**:
     a. AI can aid in environmental conservation by monitoring wildlife, detecting illegal activities like poaching and deforestation, and predicting natural disasters to enhance preparedness and response.
6. **AI in Creative Arts**:
     a. AI-generated art, music, literature, and film will continue to evolve, creating new forms of expression and collaboration between humans and machines. AI could become a co-creator, enhancing human creativity.

As AI technology advances, its applications will expand, transforming industries and society in ways we are only beginning to imagine. The potential for innovation is vast, but so are the ethical considerations that must be addressed to ensure AI is developed and deployed responsibly.

Chapter 2: Ethical Challenges in AI

Bias and Fairness

How Biases in Data Can Lead to Biased AI Outcomes

Artificial Intelligence (AI) systems learn from data. When this data contains biases—whether explicit or implicit—AI can perpetuate and even amplify these biases. Bias in AI can originate from various sources, including:

1. **Historical Inequities**: If historical data reflects societal biases, AI systems trained on such data can replicate and reinforce these inequities.
2. **Sampling Bias**: If the training data does not represent the diversity of the population, AI systems may perform poorly on underrepresented groups.
3. **Labeling Bias**: Human biases in labeling training data can introduce systematic errors.
4. **Algorithmic Bias**: Algorithms themselves may have inherent biases depending on their design and the objectives set by developers.

For example, if a facial recognition system is trained predominantly on images of light-skinned individuals, it might not perform accurately on people with darker skin tones, leading to biased outcomes.

Case Studies Highlighting Instances of AI Bias

1. **COMPAS Recidivism Algorithm**:
   a. The Correctional Offender Management Profiling for Alternative Sanctions (COMPAS) algorithm was designed to predict the likelihood of a criminal reoffending. However, investigations revealed that COMPAS was biased against African Americans, consistently scoring them higher on the risk of recidivism compared to white individuals with similar backgrounds. This bias stemmed from the historical data used to train the algorithm, which reflected existing racial biases in the criminal justice system.
2. **Amazon's AI Recruitment Tool**:
   a. Amazon developed an AI recruitment tool to streamline the hiring process. However, the tool was found to be biased against women. It favored resumes that included male-dominated terms and penalized those that mentioned female-associated terms. This bias resulted from the training data, which was predominantly sourced from male-dominated industries and roles.

Strategies for Mitigating Bias in AI Systems

1. **Diverse and Representative Data**:
   a. Ensure that training data is diverse and representative of the entire population. This involves collecting data from various demographic groups and addressing any gaps or imbalances.
2. **Bias Detection and Monitoring**:

a. Implement tools and techniques to detect and monitor bias throughout the AI development lifecycle. Regularly evaluate the performance of AI systems across different demographic groups to identify and address biases.

3. **Fairness-Aware Algorithms**:
   a. Develop and use algorithms designed to be aware of and mitigate biases. Techniques such as reweighting, resampling, and adversarial debiasing can help reduce biases in AI outcomes.

4. **Human Oversight and Auditing**:
   a. Ensure human oversight in AI decision-making processes. Regular audits of AI systems by independent third parties can help identify and rectify biases.

Privacy and Surveillance

The Impact of AI on Personal Privacy

AI systems often rely on vast amounts of personal data to function effectively. This reliance raises significant privacy concerns, including:

1. **Data Collection**: AI applications, especially those in social media, online advertising, and surveillance, collect extensive personal information. This data can include location, browsing history, purchasing habits, and even biometric information.
2. **Data Storage and Security**: Storing large volumes of personal data poses security risks. Data breaches can lead to unauthorized access and misuse of sensitive information.
3. **Inference and Profiling**: AI can infer additional details about individuals based on their data, leading to detailed profiling. This profiling can be intrusive and used for purposes beyond the individual's knowledge or consent.

Ethical Concerns Regarding Surveillance and Data Collection

1. **Informed Consent**: Individuals often do not have full awareness or control over how their data is collected, stored, and used. Ensuring informed consent is crucial to maintaining ethical standards in AI.
2. **Data Ownership and Control**: Questions about who owns and controls the data collected by AI systems are central to the ethical debate. Individuals should have the right to access, correct, and delete their data.
3. **Surveillance and Civil Liberties**: AI-driven surveillance systems can infringe on civil liberties by enabling mass surveillance and intrusive monitoring. This can lead to a chilling effect on freedom of expression and other fundamental rights.

Balancing Security and Privacy in AI Applications

1. **Privacy-Preserving Techniques**: Techniques such as differential privacy, federated learning, and homomorphic encryption can help protect individual privacy while still allowing AI systems to learn from data.

2. **Transparent Data Policies**: Organizations should be transparent about their data collection and usage policies. Clear communication about what data is collected, how it is used, and for what purposes can build trust and ensure compliance with ethical standards.
3. **Regulatory Compliance**: Adhering to regulations like the General Data Protection Regulation (GDPR) can help ensure that AI applications balance security and privacy. These regulations mandate data protection principles such as data minimization, purpose limitation, and individual rights.

Accountability and Transparency

Challenges in Ensuring AI Systems Are Transparent and Accountable

1. **Complexity of AI Models**: Many AI models, particularly deep learning systems, are highly complex and operate as "black boxes." Their decision-making processes are not easily interpretable, making it difficult to understand how they arrive at specific outcomes.
2. **Lack of Standards**: There is a lack of standardized methods for auditing and verifying AI systems, which complicates efforts to ensure transparency and accountability.
3. **Responsibility and Liability**: Determining who is responsible for the actions and decisions of AI systems can be challenging, especially when these systems are autonomous and operate with minimal human intervention.

The Concept of the "Black Box" in AI Decision-Making

The "black box" problem refers to the opacity of AI systems, where the internal workings of the model are not transparent or easily understood by humans. This lack of transparency poses several challenges:

1. **Interpretability**: Without understanding how AI systems make decisions, it is difficult to interpret and trust their outputs. This is particularly problematic in high-stakes domains like healthcare, finance, and criminal justice.
2. **Accountability**: When AI systems make decisions that impact individuals' lives, it is essential to have mechanisms to hold these systems accountable. The black box nature of AI complicates efforts to assign responsibility and ensure fairness.

Approaches to Improve Transparency in AI Algorithms

1. **Explainable AI (XAI)**:
   a. Develop AI models that provide clear and understandable explanations for their decisions. Techniques like LIME (Local Interpretable Model-agnostic Explanations) and SHAP (SHapley Additive exPlanations) can help make AI outputs more interpretable.
2. **Model Documentation and Reporting**:
   a. Create detailed documentation for AI models, including their development process, training data, performance metrics, and potential biases. This

documentation should be accessible to stakeholders, including end-users, regulators, and auditors.

3. **Auditing and Testing**:
   a. Conduct regular audits and tests to evaluate the performance, fairness, and transparency of AI systems. Independent third-party audits can provide objective assessments and identify areas for improvement.

4. **Ethical AI Frameworks**:
   a. Adopt ethical AI frameworks and guidelines that emphasize transparency, accountability, and fairness. These frameworks can provide a structured approach to developing and deploying AI systems responsibly.

In summary, addressing the ethical challenges in AI requires a multifaceted approach that includes mitigating biases, protecting privacy, ensuring accountability, and enhancing transparency. By prioritizing these ethical considerations, we can develop AI systems that are fair, trustworthy, and beneficial for society.

Chapter 3: AI in Healthcare: Ethical Considerations

The Promise of AI in Healthcare

Potential Benefits of AI in Diagnosis, Treatment, and Patient Care

Artificial Intelligence (AI) holds immense potential to revolutionize healthcare, offering numerous benefits that can enhance diagnosis, treatment, and patient care:

1. **Enhanced Diagnostics**:
   a. AI algorithms can analyze medical images and data with remarkable accuracy, often surpassing human capabilities. These tools can detect diseases at early stages, improving outcomes through timely intervention. For instance, AI can identify subtle patterns in radiology images that might be missed by human eyes, aiding in the early detection of cancers, neurological disorders, and cardiovascular diseases.
2. **Personalized Treatment**:
   a. AI enables personalized medicine by analyzing a patient's genetic information, lifestyle, and medical history to tailor treatments specifically to their needs. This approach can improve the efficacy of treatments and minimize adverse effects, particularly in complex diseases like cancer where personalized treatment plans can significantly impact survival rates.
3. **Predictive Analytics**:
   a. AI-driven predictive analytics can forecast disease progression and patient outcomes, allowing healthcare providers to implement preventive measures and optimize treatment plans. For example, AI can predict which patients are at risk of complications post-surgery, enabling preemptive care strategies.
4. **Operational Efficiency**:
   a. AI can streamline administrative processes in healthcare, reducing paperwork and freeing up healthcare professionals to focus on patient care. This includes automated scheduling, electronic health record (EHR) management, and inventory management for medical supplies.
5. **Telemedicine and Remote Monitoring**:
   a. AI-powered telemedicine platforms enable remote consultations, making healthcare accessible to patients in rural or underserved areas. Additionally, AI-driven wearable devices can continuously monitor vital signs and alert healthcare providers to any abnormalities, ensuring timely medical intervention.

Examples of Successful AI Applications in Healthcare

1. **IBM Watson for Oncology**:
   a. IBM Watson uses AI to assist oncologists in making evidence-based treatment decisions. By analyzing vast amounts of medical literature and patient data, Watson provides recommendations tailored to individual patients, improving treatment accuracy and outcomes.

2. **DeepMind's AI for Eye Disease**:
    a. DeepMind, a subsidiary of Google, developed an AI system capable of diagnosing eye diseases from retinal scans with high precision. This technology aids ophthalmologists in identifying conditions like diabetic retinopathy and age-related macular degeneration early, preventing vision loss.
3. **Aidoc's Radiology Solutions**:
    a. Aidoc's AI-powered radiology solutions help radiologists detect critical findings in medical images, such as brain hemorrhages, pulmonary embolisms, and spinal fractures. These tools significantly reduce diagnostic turnaround times and improve patient care.
4. **PathAI's Histopathology**:
    a. PathAI uses AI to analyze pathology slides, assisting pathologists in diagnosing diseases like cancer more accurately and efficiently. The AI system can identify patterns and anomalies in tissue samples, ensuring precise and timely diagnoses.

Ethical Concerns

Issues of Data Privacy and Patient Consent

1. **Data Privacy**:
    a. AI systems in healthcare rely on vast amounts of patient data to train algorithms and improve accuracy. This raises significant concerns about data privacy, as sensitive health information can be vulnerable to breaches and misuse. Ensuring robust data security measures and compliance with regulations like the Health Insurance Portability and Accountability Act (HIPAA) is crucial to protect patient confidentiality.
2. **Patient Consent**:
    a. Informed consent is a fundamental ethical principle in healthcare. Patients must be fully aware of how their data will be used, stored, and shared when interacting with AI systems. Transparent communication about the benefits and risks associated with AI in healthcare is essential to maintain patient trust and autonomy.

The Role of AI in Decision-Making and the Importance of Human Oversight

1. **AI in Decision-Making**:
    a. While AI can provide valuable insights and recommendations, the final decision-making should always involve human healthcare professionals. AI systems can aid in diagnostics and treatment planning, but they should not replace the clinical judgment and expertise of doctors. Human oversight ensures that ethical considerations, individual patient circumstances, and nuanced clinical factors are taken into account.
2. **Maintaining Accountability**:

a. Clear lines of accountability must be established when AI systems are used in healthcare. It is essential to determine who is responsible for AI-driven decisions and outcomes, ensuring that healthcare providers can address any errors or adverse effects resulting from AI recommendations.

Equity and Access to AI-Driven Healthcare Solutions

1. **Addressing Disparities**:
   a. The integration of AI in healthcare has the potential to exacerbate existing disparities if not implemented equitably. Ensuring that AI technologies are accessible to all populations, including marginalized and underserved communities, is critical. This includes addressing barriers such as cost, digital literacy, and availability of necessary infrastructure.
2. **Bias in AI Systems**:
   a. AI systems can inadvertently perpetuate biases present in the training data, leading to unequal treatment and outcomes. For example, if an AI model is trained predominantly on data from a specific demographic, it may not perform as well for other groups. It is crucial to develop and test AI systems using diverse datasets to ensure fairness and equity.
3. **Ethical AI Development**:
   a. Developers and stakeholders must prioritize ethical considerations throughout the AI development lifecycle. This includes involving ethicists, healthcare professionals, and patient representatives in the design, testing, and deployment of AI systems to identify and mitigate potential ethical issues.

In conclusion, while AI holds tremendous promise in transforming healthcare by improving diagnostics, personalized treatment, and operational efficiency, it also presents significant ethical challenges. Addressing these concerns through robust data privacy measures, informed patient consent, human oversight, and equitable access is essential to harness the full potential of AI in healthcare responsibly. By prioritizing ethics, we can ensure that AI serves as a force for good, enhancing patient care and outcomes across diverse populations.

Chapter 4: Autonomous Vehicles and Ethical Dilemmas

The Rise of Autonomous Vehicles

Overview of Self-Driving Car Technology and Its Development

Autonomous vehicles, or self-driving cars, are designed to navigate and operate without human intervention. They use a combination of advanced technologies, including sensors, machine learning, and artificial intelligence, to perceive their environment, make decisions, and control vehicle movements.

Key technologies involved in self-driving cars include:

1. **Sensors**:
    a. **Lidar**: Light Detection and Ranging (Lidar) uses laser pulses to create a precise 3D map of the surroundings, detecting obstacles and measuring distances.
    b. **Radar**: Radio Detection and Ranging (Radar) uses radio waves to detect objects and their speed, providing information about the car's surroundings even in poor visibility conditions.
    c. **Cameras**: Multiple cameras placed around the vehicle capture images of the environment, enabling the detection of traffic signals, road signs, pedestrians, and other vehicles.
    d. **Ultrasonic Sensors**: These sensors detect objects close to the vehicle, assisting in parking and low-speed maneuvers.
2. **Artificial Intelligence (AI) and Machine Learning (ML)**:
    a. AI and ML algorithms process data from sensors to understand the environment, predict the behavior of other road users, and make driving decisions. These systems continuously learn and improve from real-world driving experiences.
3. **High-Definition (HD) Maps**:
    a. HD maps provide detailed information about road layouts, traffic signs, and lane markings, enhancing the vehicle's ability to navigate accurately.
4. **Control Systems**:
    a. These systems execute driving decisions, controlling acceleration, braking, and steering to ensure safe and efficient vehicle operation.

Development Timeline:

1. **Early Research (1980s-2000s)**: Initial research into autonomous driving began in the 1980s with projects like Carnegie Mellon's NavLab and the DARPA Grand Challenge. These projects demonstrated the feasibility of self-driving technology.
2. **Breakthroughs (2010s)**: Companies like Google (now Waymo), Tesla, and Uber advanced autonomous vehicle technology, conducting extensive testing and deploying prototypes on public roads.

3. **Current Developments (2020s)**: Major automakers and tech companies continue to invest in autonomous vehicle technology, with significant progress in sensor technology, AI algorithms, and real-world testing.

Potential Benefits: Safety, Efficiency, and Accessibility

1. **Safety**:
   a. **Reduction in Human Error**: Human error is a leading cause of traffic accidents. Autonomous vehicles, with their precise sensing and decision-making capabilities, can significantly reduce accidents caused by distracted driving, impaired driving, and other human factors.
   b. **Consistent Performance**: Unlike human drivers, autonomous vehicles do not suffer from fatigue, distraction, or emotional stress, ensuring consistent and predictable driving behavior.
2. **Efficiency**:
   a. **Optimized Traffic Flow**: Autonomous vehicles can communicate with each other and traffic infrastructure to optimize traffic flow, reduce congestion, and minimize delays.
   b. **Fuel Efficiency**: Efficient driving patterns and the potential for coordinated driving in platoons can enhance fuel efficiency and reduce emissions.
3. **Accessibility**:
   a. **Mobility for All**: Autonomous vehicles can provide mobility solutions for individuals who cannot drive, such as the elderly, disabled, or those without a driver's license. This can enhance independence and access to essential services.
   b. **Shared Mobility**: Autonomous vehicles can support shared mobility services, reducing the need for individual car ownership and promoting more sustainable urban transportation systems.

Ethical Dilemmas

Decision-Making in Life-and-Death Situations: The Trolley Problem

One of the most discussed ethical dilemmas in the context of autonomous vehicles is the "trolley problem." This philosophical thought experiment poses a moral decision-making scenario where a person (or in this case, an autonomous vehicle) must choose between two undesirable outcomes, often involving life-and-death decisions.

1. **Scenario**:
   a. An autonomous vehicle encounters a situation where a collision is unavoidable. It must decide whether to:
      i. Swerve and potentially harm a pedestrian, or
      ii. Stay on course and potentially harm the vehicle's occupants.
2. **Ethical Considerations**:

    a. **Utilitarian Approach**: This approach suggests choosing the action that results in the least harm overall. However, implementing this in autonomous vehicles raises questions about how to quantify harm and whose lives are prioritized.

    b. **Deontological Approach**: This perspective focuses on following ethical principles or rules, such as not intentionally causing harm. It challenges the vehicle to adhere to predefined ethical guidelines without considering the outcome's consequences.

3. **Challenges**:
   a. **Programming Ethics**: How should developers program ethical decision-making into autonomous vehicles? What ethical frameworks should guide these decisions?
   b. **Public Acceptance**: How will society accept the ethical decisions made by autonomous vehicles? Transparency and public engagement are crucial in gaining trust.

Liability and Responsibility in the Event of Accidents

1. **Determining Liability**:
   a. **Manufacturer Responsibility**: If an autonomous vehicle malfunctions or makes a poor decision due to a flaw in its design or programming, the manufacturer may be held liable.
   b. **Software Developers**: Liability may extend to the developers of the AI algorithms and software that control the vehicle.
   c. **Vehicle Owner/Operator**: In cases where the vehicle owner or operator failed to maintain the vehicle or tampered with its systems, they might share liability.

2. **Insurance and Legal Frameworks**:
   a. **Insurance Models**: Traditional insurance models may need to be revised to accommodate the complexities of autonomous vehicles. This could involve new types of coverage, such as product liability insurance.
   b. **Legal Regulations**: Governments and regulatory bodies must establish clear legal frameworks defining liability and accountability in autonomous vehicle accidents.

3. **Ethical Responsibility**:
   a. **Moral Accountability**: Beyond legal liability, there are questions about moral accountability. Who is ethically responsible for the actions of an autonomous vehicle? Developers, manufacturers, and users may all share some level of moral responsibility.

Regulatory and Policy Challenges

1. **Developing Standards and Regulations**:
   a. **Safety Standards**: Establishing robust safety standards for autonomous vehicles is critical. These standards must ensure that vehicles are thoroughly tested and proven safe before deployment.

    b. **Data Privacy**: Regulations must address the collection, storage, and use of data by autonomous vehicles to protect individuals' privacy and prevent misuse.

2. **Testing and Certification**:
    a. **Real-World Testing**: Autonomous vehicles must undergo extensive real-world testing to ensure they can handle a wide range of scenarios. Regulations should specify testing requirements and criteria for certification.
    b. **Continuous Monitoring**: Even after deployment, autonomous vehicles should be continuously monitored to ensure they operate safely and as intended.

3. **Ethical Guidelines**:
    a. **Transparent Decision-Making**: Regulations should require transparency in how autonomous vehicles make ethical decisions, including public disclosure of the decision-making frameworks used.
    b. **Public Engagement**: Policymakers should engage with the public to understand societal values and preferences regarding autonomous vehicle ethics.

4. **International Coordination**:
    a. **Harmonized Regulations**: As autonomous vehicles operate across borders, international coordination is essential to harmonize regulations and ensure consistent safety and ethical standards globally.

In conclusion, while autonomous vehicles promise significant benefits in terms of safety, efficiency, and accessibility, they also present complex ethical dilemmas. Addressing these challenges requires careful consideration of bias and fairness, privacy and surveillance, accountability and transparency, and a collaborative effort between technologists, ethicists, policymakers, and the public. By prioritizing ethical principles and robust regulatory frameworks, we can harness the potential of autonomous vehicles responsibly and equitably.

Chapter 5: AI and Employment: Opportunities and Risks

AI's Impact on the Job Market

Potential for Job Displacement and the Creation of New Roles

Artificial Intelligence (AI) is transforming industries and redefining the nature of work. This transformation brings both opportunities and risks:

1. **Job Displacement**:
   a. **Automation of Routine Tasks**: AI and robotics can automate repetitive and mundane tasks, which may lead to job displacement in sectors like manufacturing, retail, and administrative services. For example, automated checkout systems in retail and robotic process automation in administrative tasks can replace human roles.
   b. **Impact on Low-Skill Jobs**: Jobs that require low to moderate levels of skill and involve predictable physical or cognitive activities are particularly vulnerable to automation. This includes roles such as data entry clerks, assembly line workers, and telemarketers.
2. **Creation of New Roles**:
   a. **Emergence of New Industries**: AI will create entirely new industries and business models. For instance, the development and maintenance of AI systems require expertise in AI research, data science, machine learning engineering, and AI ethics.
   b. **Enhanced Job Functions**: AI can augment existing roles by taking over routine tasks, allowing workers to focus on more complex, creative, and strategic activities. For example, AI can assist doctors with diagnostic tasks, enabling them to spend more time on patient care and treatment planning.
   c. **Shift in Job Demand**: As AI adoption grows, there will be increased demand for roles that support AI technologies, such as AI trainers, data labelers, and algorithm auditors.

Sectors Most Likely to Be Affected by AI Automation

1. **Manufacturing**:
   a. **Robotics and Automation**: AI-driven robots and automated systems can perform assembly line tasks, quality control, and predictive maintenance, leading to significant changes in manufacturing operations.
2. **Retail**:
   a. **Automated Checkout and Inventory Management**: AI-powered systems can manage inventory, automate checkouts, and provide personalized shopping experiences through recommendation engines.
3. **Healthcare**:

a. **Diagnostics and Administrative Tasks**: AI can assist in diagnostic imaging, patient data analysis, and administrative tasks like scheduling and billing, improving efficiency and accuracy.
4. **Finance**:
   a. **Algorithmic Trading and Fraud Detection**: AI algorithms can execute high-frequency trading strategies, analyze market trends, and detect fraudulent activities in financial transactions.
5. **Transportation and Logistics**:
   a. **Autonomous Vehicles and Delivery Drones**: AI is driving the development of autonomous vehicles and drones for transportation and logistics, potentially reducing the need for human drivers and delivery personnel.
6. **Customer Service**:
   a. **Chatbots and Virtual Assistants**: AI-powered chatbots and virtual assistants can handle customer inquiries, support, and service requests, reducing the need for human customer service representatives.

Ethical Considerations

Ensuring a Fair Transition for Displaced Workers

1. **Supportive Policies**:
   a. **Unemployment Benefits**: Governments should provide adequate unemployment benefits to support workers who lose their jobs due to AI-driven automation.
   b. **Job Placement Services**: Initiatives to help displaced workers find new employment opportunities, such as job placement services and career counseling, are crucial.
2. **Corporate Responsibility**:
   a. **Employee Transition Programs**: Companies should invest in transition programs for employees affected by automation, including severance packages, retraining programs, and assistance in finding new roles within or outside the organization.
3. **Social Safety Nets**:
   a. **Basic Income**: Some propose the idea of a universal basic income (UBI) as a safety net for individuals affected by job displacement due to AI. UBI would provide a guaranteed income to help individuals meet their basic needs while they transition to new employment.

The Role of Education and Retraining in an AI-Driven Economy

1. **Continuous Learning**:
   a. **Lifelong Learning Programs**: Governments and organizations should promote lifelong learning initiatives to help workers continuously update their skills and remain competitive in an AI-driven job market.

b. **Online Learning Platforms**: Platforms like Coursera, edX, and Udacity offer courses in AI, data science, and other emerging fields, enabling individuals to acquire new skills at their own pace.

2. **Reskilling and Upskilling**:
   a. **Technical Training**: Programs focused on reskilling and upskilling workers in technical fields such as AI, machine learning, and data analysis can help bridge the skills gap.
   b. **Soft Skills Development**: In addition to technical skills, there should be an emphasis on developing soft skills such as critical thinking, problem-solving, and adaptability, which are essential in an AI-driven economy.

3. **Educational Institutions**:
   a. **Curriculum Updates**: Educational institutions should update their curricula to include AI-related subjects and ensure that students are prepared for the future job market.
   b. **Industry Partnerships**: Collaboration between educational institutions and industry can create programs that align with current job market demands and provide students with practical experience.

Balancing Productivity Gains with Social Equity

1. **Equitable Distribution of AI Benefits**:
   a. **Inclusive Growth**: Policies should ensure that the economic benefits of AI-driven productivity gains are distributed equitably across society. This includes investing in public services, education, and infrastructure.
   b. **Fair Wages**: Ensuring that workers in AI-augmented roles receive fair wages and benefits is crucial for maintaining social equity.

2. **Corporate Responsibility**:
   a. **Ethical AI Development**: Companies should prioritize the ethical development and deployment of AI technologies, considering their impact on employment and society.
   b. **Stakeholder Engagement**: Engaging with stakeholders, including employees, customers, and communities, can help companies understand the broader social implications of AI and develop responsible strategies.

3. **Government Intervention**:
   a. **Regulation and Oversight**: Governments should establish regulations and oversight mechanisms to ensure that AI technologies are developed and used ethically, with a focus on protecting workers' rights and promoting social equity.
   b. **Investment in Social Programs**: Investing in social programs that support education, healthcare, and community development can help mitigate the negative impacts of AI-driven job displacement.

In conclusion, while AI presents significant opportunities for enhancing productivity and creating new job roles, it also poses risks related to job displacement and social equity. Addressing these challenges requires a comprehensive approach that includes supportive policies for displaced workers, investment in education and retraining, and a commitment to equitable growth. By prioritizing ethical considerations and social responsibility, we can harness the potential of AI to create a more inclusive and prosperous future.

Chapter 6: Governance and Regulation of AI

The Need for Regulation

Why AI Needs Oversight and Regulation

Artificial Intelligence (AI) has the potential to revolutionize various sectors, driving innovation and enhancing efficiency. However, the rapid advancement and widespread adoption of AI technologies also pose significant risks and ethical challenges, necessitating oversight and regulation:

1. **Preventing Harm**:
    a. AI systems can impact critical areas such as healthcare, transportation, and finance. Ensuring these systems operate safely and reliably is crucial to prevent harm to individuals and society.
    b. Example: In healthcare, AI diagnostic tools must be thoroughly validated to avoid misdiagnoses that could lead to incorrect treatments.
2. **Ensuring Fairness and Equity**:
    a. AI can perpetuate and amplify biases present in training data, leading to unfair and discriminatory outcomes.
    b. Example: Biased AI hiring algorithms can disadvantage certain demographic groups, perpetuating existing inequalities.
3. **Protecting Privacy**:
    a. AI systems often rely on vast amounts of personal data, raising concerns about data privacy and surveillance.
    b. Example: AI-driven surveillance systems can infringe on individual privacy rights and lead to unwarranted surveillance.
4. **Accountability and Transparency**:
    a. The complexity and opacity of AI systems, often referred to as "black boxes," make it difficult to understand their decision-making processes, leading to challenges in ensuring accountability and transparency.
    b. Example: Autonomous vehicles need clear accountability frameworks to determine responsibility in the event of accidents.
5. **Mitigating Ethical Concerns**:
    a. AI technologies raise ethical questions about their impact on employment, human rights, and societal values.
    b. Example: Autonomous weapons systems pose ethical dilemmas regarding their use in warfare and the potential for unintended consequences.

Key Principles for Ethical AI Governance

1. **Fairness**:
    a. AI systems should be designed and deployed to ensure fair treatment of all individuals, avoiding biases and discrimination.

b. Implement measures such as bias detection, diverse training data, and fairness-aware algorithms.
2. **Transparency**:
   a. AI systems should be transparent in their operations, providing clear explanations for their decisions.
   b. Encourage the development of explainable AI (XAI) and require documentation and disclosure of AI decision-making processes.
3. **Accountability**:
   a. Clear mechanisms should be established to hold individuals and organizations accountable for the outcomes of AI systems.
   b. Define legal and ethical responsibilities for AI developers, users, and manufacturers.
4. **Privacy and Data Protection**:
   a. AI systems must respect individual privacy rights and ensure the secure handling of personal data.
   b. Implement data protection measures such as encryption, anonymization, and compliance with data protection regulations.
5. **Safety and Reliability**:
   a. AI systems should be rigorously tested and validated to ensure they operate safely and reliably in real-world conditions.
   b. Establish safety standards and certification processes for AI technologies.
6. **Human-Centered Approach**:
   a. AI development and deployment should prioritize human well-being and societal benefits.
   b. Engage with stakeholders, including the public, to understand their concerns and values.

Existing Frameworks and Proposals

Overview of Current Regulatory Approaches in Different Countries

1. **European Union (EU)**:
   a. The EU has been proactive in developing comprehensive AI regulations. The proposed AI Act aims to create a legal framework for trustworthy AI, categorizing AI applications into different risk levels and setting requirements for high-risk AI systems.
   b. Key elements include transparency obligations, oversight mechanisms, and stringent requirements for high-risk AI applications.
2. **United States (US)**:
   a. The US has taken a more sector-specific approach, with agencies like the Federal Trade Commission (FTC) and the Food and Drug Administration (FDA) providing guidance on AI applications in their respective domains.
   b. Legislative efforts, such as the Algorithmic Accountability Act, aim to address AI biases and promote transparency.
3. **China**:

a. China has focused on AI as a strategic priority, with significant investments in AI research and development. The government has issued guidelines to promote ethical AI, emphasizing security, controllability, and fairness.
b. Regulatory measures include guidelines for autonomous vehicles, facial recognition technology, and data privacy.
4. **Canada**:
    a. Canada has adopted the Pan-Canadian AI Strategy, which emphasizes ethical AI development and responsible innovation. The Canadian government has also introduced the Digital Charter, focusing on data privacy and trust in digital technologies.
5. **Japan**:
    a. Japan's AI strategy emphasizes human-centered AI and international collaboration. The government has developed guidelines for ethical AI, promoting transparency, fairness, and accountability.

International Efforts to Establish AI Ethics Guidelines

1. **OECD Principles on AI**:
    a. The Organisation for Economic Co-operation and Development (OECD) has established AI principles that focus on promoting AI that is innovative, trustworthy, and respects human rights and democratic values. The principles include recommendations on transparency, accountability, and robust AI governance.
2. **G20 AI Principles**:
    a. The G20 has endorsed AI principles that align with the OECD guidelines, emphasizing human-centered AI, inclusivity, and international cooperation.
3. **UNESCO Recommendation on the Ethics of AI**:
    a. UNESCO has developed a recommendation on the ethics of AI, aiming to guide the development and use of AI technologies in ways that respect human rights, promote sustainability, and foster inclusive societies.
4. **Global Partnership on AI (GPAI)**:
    a. GPAI is an international initiative that brings together experts from governments, industry, academia, and civil society to collaborate on AI research and policy development. The partnership focuses on responsible AI development, human rights, and international cooperation.

Future Directions

Potential Developments in AI Governance

1. **Adaptive Regulations**:
    a. AI governance will likely evolve to become more adaptive, allowing for flexible and responsive regulatory frameworks that can keep pace with rapid technological advancements. This may involve the use of regulatory sandboxes, where AI innovations can be tested in controlled environments.

2. **Ethical AI Standards**:
    a. The development and adoption of global ethical AI standards will be crucial in ensuring consistent and responsible AI practices across different regions and industries. These standards could address issues such as bias, transparency, and accountability.
3. **AI Impact Assessments**:
    a. Similar to environmental impact assessments, AI impact assessments could become a standard practice, requiring organizations to evaluate and disclose the potential social, ethical, and economic impacts of their AI systems before deployment.
4. **AI Certification Programs**:
    a. Certification programs for AI systems could be established, ensuring that AI technologies meet predefined ethical and safety standards before they are allowed on the market.

The Role of Global Cooperation in Regulating AI

1. **Harmonized Regulations**:
    a. International cooperation is essential for harmonizing AI regulations, ensuring that AI systems developed in one country can be safely and ethically deployed in others. Harmonized regulations can prevent regulatory arbitrage, where companies exploit differences in regulations between countries.
2. **Cross-Border Data Governance**:
    a. AI systems often rely on cross-border data flows. International agreements on data governance can ensure that data is handled ethically and securely, respecting privacy and sovereignty concerns.
3. **Collaborative Research and Development**:
    a. Global cooperation in AI research and development can promote shared knowledge, resources, and best practices. Collaborative efforts can drive innovation while addressing global challenges such as climate change, healthcare, and social inequality.
4. **International Ethical Frameworks**:
    a. Developing international ethical frameworks for AI can guide countries in creating their own regulations and policies, ensuring that AI development aligns with shared human values and principles.
5. **Addressing Global Challenges**:
    a. AI has the potential to address global challenges, but this requires coordinated international efforts. For instance, AI can contribute to achieving the United Nations Sustainable Development Goals (SDGs) by improving healthcare, education, and environmental sustainability.

In conclusion, effective governance and regulation of AI are critical to harnessing its potential while mitigating its risks. By prioritizing ethical principles, adapting regulatory frameworks, and fostering global cooperation, we can ensure that AI technologies are developed and deployed in ways that benefit society as a whole.

Conclusion: The Path Forward

As we conclude our exploration of Artificial Intelligence (AI) and its ethical implications, it's essential to reflect on the key challenges identified and consider the path forward towards responsible AI development.

Summarizing the Key Ethical Challenges and Potential Solutions

Throughout this book, we have examined several ethical challenges posed by AI technologies across various domains:

1. **Bias and Fairness**:
   a. AI systems can perpetuate biases present in training data, leading to unfair and discriminatory outcomes. Solutions include implementing bias detection algorithms, using diverse and representative datasets, and developing fairness-aware AI models.
2. **Privacy and Surveillance**:
   a. AI relies on vast amounts of personal data, raising concerns about privacy infringement and surveillance. Mitigation strategies involve adopting privacy-preserving techniques such as encryption and anonymization, and enforcing strict data protection regulations.
3. **Accountability and Transparency**:
   a. The opacity of AI decision-making processes, often referred to as the "black box" problem, challenges accountability. Enhancing transparency through explainable AI (XAI) and establishing clear frameworks for AI accountability are crucial.
4. **Safety and Reliability**:
   a. AI systems must operate safely and reliably to prevent harm to individuals and society. Rigorous testing, validation, and adherence to safety standards are essential to ensure AI systems perform as intended without unexpected failures.
5. **Impact on Employment**:
   a. AI automation has the potential to displace jobs while creating new roles. Ensuring a fair transition for displaced workers through retraining programs, supportive policies, and promoting lifelong learning is essential to mitigate socio-economic impacts.
6. **Governance and Regulation**:
   a. The need for robust AI governance and regulation is critical to address ethical concerns and ensure AI technologies are developed and deployed responsibly. This includes establishing ethical principles, adapting regulatory frameworks, and fostering global cooperation.

The Importance of Ongoing Dialogue and Collaboration Among Stakeholders

Addressing these ethical challenges requires ongoing dialogue and collaboration among diverse stakeholders:

1. **Multidisciplinary Approach**:
   a. Collaboration between technologists, ethicists, policymakers, educators, and civil society is essential to develop holistic solutions that consider technical, ethical, legal, and societal perspectives.
2. **Engaging the Public**:
   a. Public engagement is crucial to understanding societal values, concerns, and expectations regarding AI technologies. Open dialogue can foster trust, transparency, and accountability in AI development and deployment.
3. **Industry Leadership**:
   a. Industry leaders have a responsibility to prioritize ethical considerations in AI development, integrating ethical guidelines into their organizational culture, and advocating for responsible AI practices across the sector.
4. **Government Regulation**:
   a. Governments play a pivotal role in establishing regulatory frameworks that promote ethical AI, protect public interests, and ensure compliance with legal and ethical standards.

Encouraging Responsible AI Development for the Benefit of Society

Moving forward, it is imperative to encourage responsible AI development that maximizes societal benefits while minimizing risks:

1. **Ethical by Design**:
   a. Adopting a "design for ethics" approach ensures that ethical considerations are embedded into the design, development, and deployment phases of AI technologies.
2. **Continuous Ethics Review**:
   a. Implementing mechanisms for continuous ethics review and impact assessments can identify and address ethical issues throughout the lifecycle of AI systems.
3. **Education and Awareness**:
   a. Promoting AI literacy and awareness among the public, policymakers, and industry stakeholders is crucial for informed decision-making and responsible use of AI technologies.
4. **International Collaboration**:
   a. Global cooperation is essential to harmonize AI regulations, share best practices, and address cross-border ethical challenges. Initiatives like the Global Partnership on AI (GPAI) facilitate collaborative efforts towards ethical AI development.
5. **Innovation with Purpose**:
   a. Encouraging innovation that aligns with societal values and addresses pressing global challenges, such as healthcare, climate change, and social inequality, demonstrates the positive potential of AI for humanity.

In conclusion, navigating the ethical landscape of AI requires a balanced approach that prioritizes human well-being, promotes fairness and transparency, and fosters innovation in ways that benefit society as a whole. By embracing ethical principles and fostering collaborative efforts, we can harness the transformative power of AI responsibly and ensure a future where AI technologies contribute positively to our collective well-being.

Appendix

Further Reading and Resources

For readers interested in delving deeper into the intersection of Artificial Intelligence (AI) and ethics, the following books, articles, and websites offer valuable insights and perspectives:

Books:

1. *Weapons of Math Destruction: How Big Data Increases Inequality and Threatens Democracy* by Cathy O'Neil
2. *Artificial Intelligence: A Guide for Thinking Humans* by Melanie Mitchell
3. *AI Superpowers: China, Silicon Valley, and the New World Order* by Kai-Fu Lee
4. *Artificial Intelligence: What Everyone Needs to Know* by Jerry Kaplan
5. *Ethics of Artificial Intelligence and Robotics* edited by Vincent C. Müller and Nick Bostrom

Articles:

1. "The Malicious Use of Artificial Intelligence: Forecasting, Prevention, and Mitigation" - Future of Humanity Institute, University of Oxford
2. "The Ethics of Artificial Intelligence" - Stanford Encyclopedia of Philosophy
3. "Fairness and Abstraction in Sociotechnical Systems" - Communications of the ACM
4. "The Rise of the Ethical Machines" - Harvard Business Review
5. "The Future of AI Regulation" - Brookings Institution

Websites:

1. **AI Ethics**: Resources and articles on AI ethics from the Future of Life Institute - futureoflife.org/ai-ethics
2. **Ethics & Society Blog**: Insights and discussions on AI ethics from the Markkula Center for Applied Ethics - scu.edu/ethics/ethics-resources/ethics-blog/
3. **AI and Society**: Articles and research on the societal impacts of AI from the AI and Society journal - springer.com/journal/146
4. **AI Now Institute**: Research and reports on the social implications of AI from New York University - ainowinstitute.org
5. **IEEE Global Initiative on Ethics of Autonomous and Intelligent Systems**: Standards and resources on ethical AI development from the Institute of Electrical and Electronics Engineers - standards.ieee.org/industry-connections/ec/autonomous-systems.html

Glossary of Terms

Artificial Intelligence (AI): A branch of computer science that focuses on creating systems capable of performing tasks that would typically require human intelligence.

Machine Learning: A subset of AI that enables machines to learn from data and improve their performance over time without being explicitly programmed.

Deep Learning: A subset of machine learning that uses artificial neural networks with many layers (hence "deep") to learn from large amounts of data.

Algorithm: A set of rules or instructions followed by a computer to solve a problem or achieve a specific task.

Bias: Systematic errors or inaccuracies in data or algorithms that result in unfair or discriminatory outcomes.

Transparency: The quality of AI systems being understandable and explainable, particularly in their decision-making processes.

Privacy: The right of individuals to control their personal information and how it is collected, used, and shared by others.

Ethics: Principles and standards of conduct that guide decisions and behaviors, especially concerning what is right and wrong.

Accountability: The responsibility of individuals, organizations, or systems for their actions and the consequences of those actions.

Regulation: Rules and guidelines established by governments or authorities to control and manage the behavior and development of AI technologies.

References

The information presented in this book is supported by the following references and citations:

1. Cathy O'Neil, *Weapons of Math Destruction: How Big Data Increases Inequality and Threatens Democracy*
2. Melanie Mitchell, *Artificial Intelligence: A Guide for Thinking Humans*
3. Kai-Fu Lee, *AI Superpowers: China, Silicon Valley, and the New World Order*
4. Jerry Kaplan, *Artificial Intelligence: What Everyone Needs to Know*
5. Vincent C. Müller and Nick Bostrom (Eds.), *Ethics of Artificial Intelligence and Robotics*

For specific articles and online resources, please refer to the respective websites and sources mentioned in the Further Reading section above. These sources provide comprehensive insights and research on the ethical implications of AI, contributing to a deeper understanding of this rapidly evolving field.